EXPLORATION
of MARS

Author and artist:

Mark Bergin studied at Eastbourne College of Art and has specialised in historical reconstructions, aviation and maritime subjects since 1983. He has been commissioned by aerospace companies and has illustrated a number of books on flight and space. He lives in Bexhill-on-Sea with his wife and three children.

Consultant:

Carole Stott is a full-time science writer. She was formerly Curator of Astronomy and then Head of Observatory at the Royal Observatory, Greenwich. She has written more than 20 books for both children and adults and has contributed to numerous encyclopedias and science publications.

Series creator:

David Salariya was born in Dundee, Scotland. He has illustrated a wide range of titles and has created many new series of books for publishers in the UK and overseas. In 1989 he established The Salariya Book Company. He lives in Brighton with his wife, illustrator Shirley Willis, and their son Jonathan.

Editors:

Karen Barker Smith
Stephanie Cole

Published in Great Britain in 2002
by Book House, an imprint of
The Salariya Book Company Ltd
25 Marlborough Place, Brighton BN1 1UB

The Salariya
Book Co. Ltd

Visit the Salariya Book Company at:
www.salariya.com
www.book-house.co.uk

ISBN 1 904194 34 6

A catalogue record for this book is available from the British Library.

Printed and bound in China.

Printed on paper from sustainable forests.

EXPLORATION
of MARS

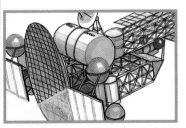

Written and illustrated by
MARK BERGIN

Created and designed by
DAVID SALARIYA

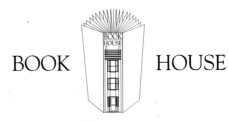

BOOK HOUSE

Contents

The Red Planet: Myth and Legend

For thousands of years, Mars has gripped the human imagination. It is different from most of the other planets in our solar system, because it moves in one direction across the night sky for several months and then appears to reverse its course and move backwards. The ancient Egyptians called Mars the 'backwards traveller'. The Greeks called the planet Ares, after their god of war, due to its strange movement and blood-red colour, which suggested doom and disorder in the heavens. The Romans renamed the planet after their own god of war, Mars – the name we still use today.

Mars, Roman god of war

Mars, the Roman god of war, was always portrayed in the armour and weapons of a soldier. The Romans made offerings and prayed to him for success in battle.

In 1543, the astronomer Nicolaus Copernicus published his theory that the planets in our solar system orbit around the sun. Until then, people thought the entire universe revolved around Earth. However, Mars' unusual orbit was difficult to explain until a German mathematician, Johannes Kepler, studied its motion. In 1609 he announced that Mars had an orbit that was an ellipse, not a circle.

Johannes Kepler

In 1877, Giovanni Schiaparelli, an Italian astronomer, made drawings and maps of the Martian surface that suggested strange features (right). The images from telescopes at this time were not as sharp as today's. Schiaparelli said he could see a network of lines, or *canali* (Italian for 'canals' or 'channels').

Giovanni Schiaparelli and his chart of Mars' canali

Percival Lowell

In 1894, an American astronomer, Percival Lowell, made a series of observations of Mars from his own observatory at Flagstaff, Arizona, USA. Lowell was convinced a great network of canals had been dug to irrigate crops for the Martian race! He suggested that each canal had fertile vegetation on either side, making them noticeable from Earth. Drawings and globes he made show a network of canals and oases all over the planet (left).

The idea that there was intelligent life on Mars gained strength in the late 19th century. In 1898, H.G. Wells wrote a science fiction classic, *The War of the Worlds*, about an invading force of Martians who try to conquer Earth. In 1917, Edgar Rice Burroughs wrote the first in a series of 11 novels about Mars. Strange beings and rampaging Martian monsters gripped the public's imagination.

A radio broadcast by Orson Welles on Halloween night in 1938 of *The War of the Worlds* caused widespread panic across America. People ran into the streets in their pyjamas – millions believed the dramatic reports of a Martian invasion!

In 1976, the Viking 1 Mars orbiter took two images of a region of the planet commonly called 'The Face of Mars' (below). The pictures showed what looked like a human face carved out of the surface. Many UFO watchers were convinced intelligent creatures had constructed 'The Face'. New images from the Mars Global Surveyor in 1998 showed that the area is actually a series of eroded ridges. Odd lighting was blamed for the original images.

In the 1950s, at the beginning of the space age, there was a boom in science fiction stories about alien races and terrifying creatures from Mars and other planets. Comic book creators let their imaginations run wild!

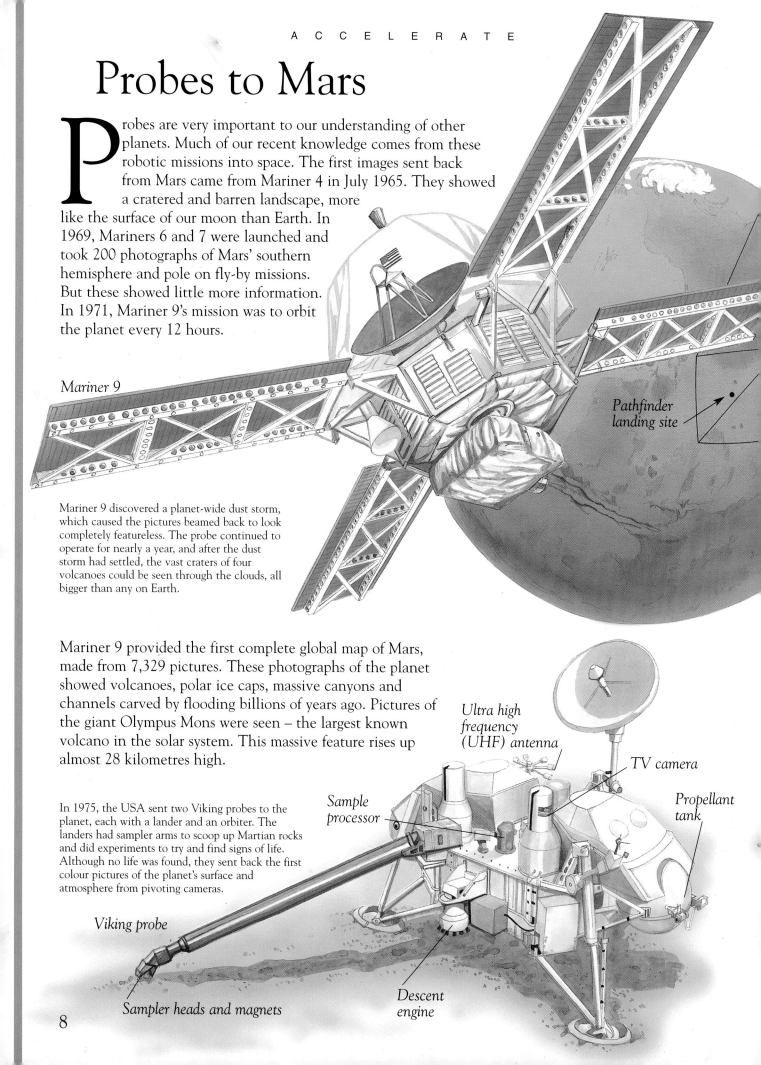

Probes to Mars

Probes are very important to our understanding of other planets. Much of our recent knowledge comes from these robotic missions into space. The first images sent back from Mars came from Mariner 4 in July 1965. They showed a cratered and barren landscape, more like the surface of our moon than Earth. In 1969, Mariners 6 and 7 were launched and took 200 photographs of Mars' southern hemisphere and pole on fly-by missions. But these showed little more information. In 1971, Mariner 9's mission was to orbit the planet every 12 hours.

Mariner 9

Mariner 9 discovered a planet-wide dust storm, which caused the pictures beamed back to look completely featureless. The probe continued to operate for nearly a year, and after the dust storm had settled, the vast craters of four volcanoes could be seen through the clouds, all bigger than any on Earth.

Pathfinder landing site

Mariner 9 provided the first complete global map of Mars, made from 7,329 pictures. These photographs of the planet showed volcanoes, polar ice caps, massive canyons and channels carved by flooding billions of years ago. Pictures of the giant Olympus Mons were seen – the largest known volcano in the solar system. This massive feature rises up almost 28 kilometres high.

In 1975, the USA sent two Viking probes to the planet, each with a lander and an orbiter. The landers had sampler arms to scoop up Martian rocks and did experiments to try and find signs of life. Although no life was found, they sent back the first colour pictures of the planet's surface and atmosphere from pivoting cameras.

Ultra high frequency (UHF) antenna

TV camera

Sample processor

Propellant tank

Viking probe

Sampler heads and magnets

Descent engine

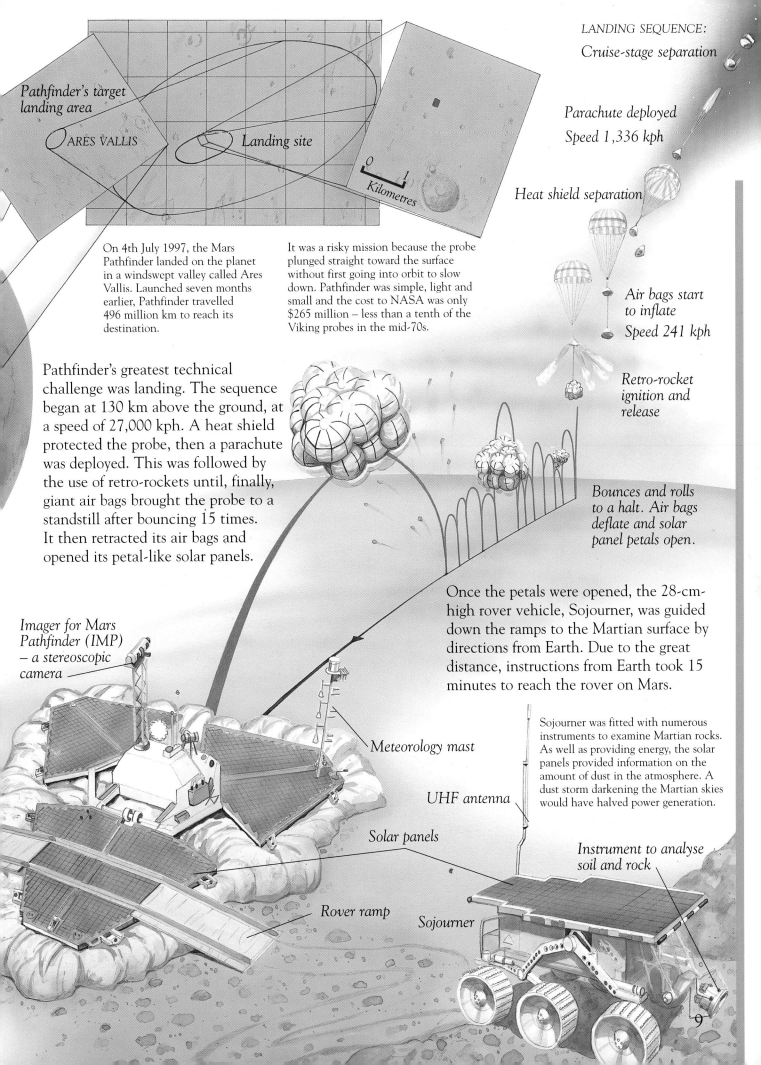

Pathfinder's target
landing area

ARES VALLIS   Landing site

0   1
Kilometres

Parachute deployed
Speed 1,336 kph

Heat shield separation

Air bags start
to inflate
Speed 241 kph

Retro-rocket
ignition and
release

On 4th July 1997, the Mars Pathfinder landed on the planet in a windswept valley called Ares Vallis. Launched seven months earlier, Pathfinder travelled 496 million km to reach its destination.

It was a risky mission because the probe plunged straight toward the surface without first going into orbit to slow down. Pathfinder was simple, light and small and the cost to NASA was only $265 million – less than a tenth of the Viking probes in the mid-70s.

Pathfinder's greatest technical challenge was landing. The sequence began at 130 km above the ground, at a speed of 27,000 kph. A heat shield protected the probe, then a parachute was deployed. This was followed by the use of retro-rockets until, finally, giant air bags brought the probe to a standstill after bouncing 15 times. It then retracted its air bags and opened its petal-like solar panels.

Bounces and rolls to a halt. Air bags deflate and solar panel petals open.

Once the petals were opened, the 28-cm-high rover vehicle, Sojourner, was guided down the ramps to the Martian surface by directions from Earth. Due to the great distance, instructions from Earth took 15 minutes to reach the rover on Mars.

Imager for Mars
Pathfinder (IMP)
– a stereoscopic
camera

Sojourner was fitted with numerous instruments to examine Martian rocks. As well as providing energy, the solar panels provided information on the amount of dust in the atmosphere. A dust storm darkening the Martian skies would have halved power generation.

Meteorology mast

UHF antenna

Solar panels

Instrument to analyse
soil and rock

Rover ramp   Sojourner

9

Future Probes

Over the next decade, at least four landers and four orbiters will be sent to Mars. This small invasion fleet will hope to settle many questions on climate, geology, hydrology and whether life ever existed or flourished on the planet. One lander will use a highly sophisticated rover to collect samples of rock, which will be returned to Earth. Missions like these will lay the groundwork for future human exploration of Mars, which could take place as soon as 2020.

Mars Express

Mars Express will be the first mission to the red planet by the European Space Agency (ESA). A 60-kg lander called Beagle 2 will explore Mars' atmosphere and surface, map the planet and search for water. One of Beagle 2's main aims will be to determine whether life exists or has ever existed on the planet. Mars Express will be launched by a Soyuz Fregat rocket in June 2003.

France and the USA have both designed separate balloons that could travel over the Martian landscape. The French balloon is designed to rise in the day as the sun warms the balloon's gases. Then, as the atmosphere cools at night, the balloon will sink back to the surface.

French-designed balloon

US Mars Aerial Platform

The US Mars Aerial Platform (MAP) uses several high-pressured balloons that will fly cameras over the surface.

Below, a solar-powered rover can be seen looking for rock samples. The MISR (Mars ISRU [In Situ Resources Utilization] Sample Return) mission is planned for 2005 and could send back samples to Earth by 2008. Examining such samples is the only way to prove or disprove that there is life on Mars. It is hoped that rock, soil and atmospheric gases will be brought back to Earth. It is planned that the lander vehicle will produce its own rocket fuel from the Martian atmosphere for the return journey to Earth. It could take up to 580 days to make enough to fill the fuel tanks.

Solar-powered rover

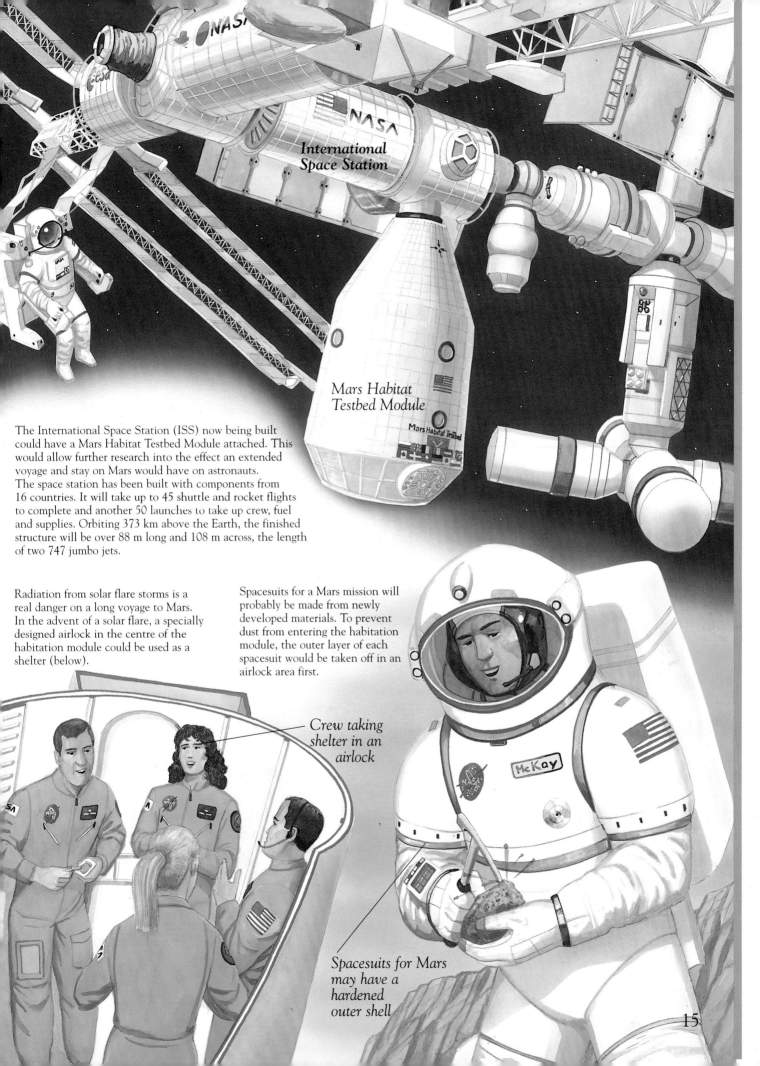

International Space Station

Mars Habitat Testbed Module

The International Space Station (ISS) now being built could have a Mars Habitat Testbed Module attached. This would allow further research into the effect an extended voyage and stay on Mars would have on astronauts. The space station has been built with components from 16 countries. It will take up to 45 shuttle and rocket flights to complete and another 50 launches to take up crew, fuel and supplies. Orbiting 373 km above the Earth, the finished structure will be over 88 m long and 108 m across, the length of two 747 jumbo jets.

Radiation from solar flare storms is a real danger on a long voyage to Mars. In the advent of a solar flare, a specially designed airlock in the centre of the habitation module could be used as a shelter (below).

Spacesuits for a Mars mission will probably be made from newly developed materials. To prevent dust from entering the habitation module, the outer layer of each spacesuit would be taken off in an airlock area first.

Crew taking shelter in an airlock

Spacesuits for Mars may have a hardened outer shell

15

Plans to Reach Mars

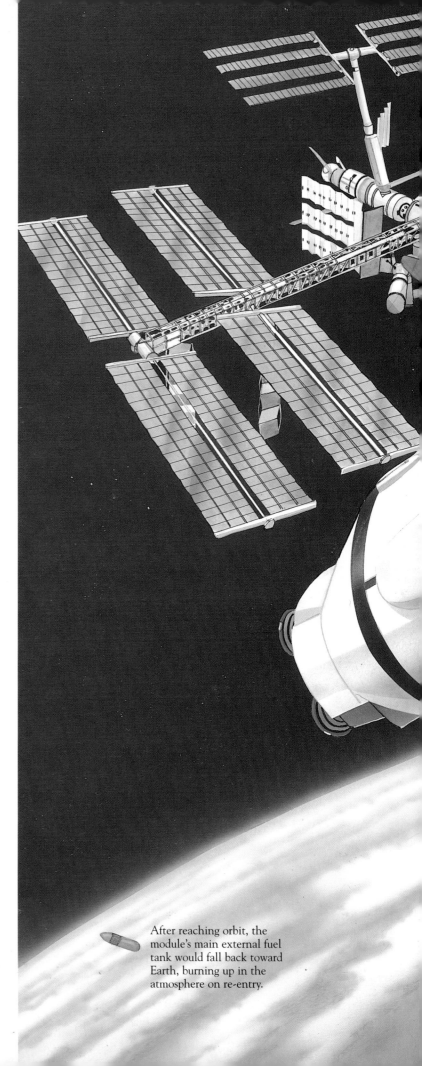

At its greatest distance from Earth, Mars is 1,000 times farther away than the moon. On the 20th anniversary of the first moon landing, in 1989, US president George Bush asked NASA to create a plan to put people on Mars. NASA came up with a 30-year plan, using similar methods developed for earlier Apollo missions. A massive interplanetary spacecraft was planned, which would have to be built outside the Earth's atmosphere at the amazing price of $450 billion! A cheaper solution was needed!

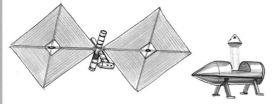

An idea from Russia for a Mars mission included the use of electric rocket motors powered by giant solar panels (above). It would make slow progress – for a two-year round trip, the astronauts would only spend one week on Mars.

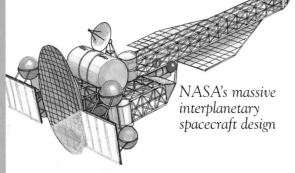

NASA's massive interplanetary spacecraft design

NASA's planned spacecraft is too expensive, so the space research community has been looking at alternatives. They have come up with two main options: Mars Semi Direct and Mars Direct.

Mars Semi Direct spacecraft design

After reaching orbit, the module's main external fuel tank would fall back toward Earth, burning up in the atmosphere on re-entry.

Once the two parts of the Mars vehicle are assembled and checked, they will blast away from Earth's orbit to start the long interplanetary journey. It will take six to nine months to reach Mars, depending on the chosen flight path.

The Mars Direct plan includes using Mars itself to provide the rocket fuel for the trip home. This would save the enormous cost of taking all the required fuel on board and would mean the spacecraft could be smaller and lighter. The technology needed to distill the Martian atmosphere into fuel has been developed but it cannot be properly tested until a mission reaches Mars. Reusing the rockets that propelled the current space shuttles or using the existing Russian Energia rocket would also reduce the cost of the mission. This would result in five Mars Direct missions costing about $40 billion – a lot cheaper than NASA's original 30-year plan. The main difference between the proposed Mars Direct and Mars Semi Direct plans is that the Semi Direct mission involves a Crew Transfer Vehicle staying in Mars' orbit.

Manned module

Shuttle and rocket parts from the space shuttle program could be reused to carry stages of a Mars mission. These parts could then be united in orbit around Earth and sent on to Mars. Another idea is an Ares booster rocket, which has been designed to fire a payload directly into interplanetary space.

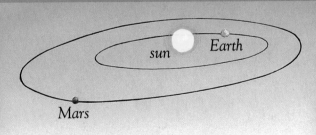

sun *Earth*

Mars

Calculating the relative positions of Earth and Mars in their orbits is essential for a successful mission to Mars. In the Mars Direct plan, a 40-tonne unmanned propellant plant (a robotic fuel-making factory) would be sent ahead. Once landed on Mars, the craft would begin pumping atmospheric gases into a reaction chamber. Mars' air is 95% carbon dioxide, and this would be exposed to hydrogen to make methane, water and oxygen, which are combined to make rocket fuel.

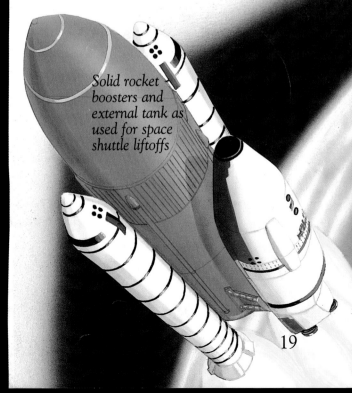

Solid rocket boosters and external tank as used for space shuttle liftoffs

19

Landing on Mars

In the Mars Direct plan, the journey to Mars will take about six months (180 days) and the astronauts will have to survive a long period of weightlessness. Rotating the spacecraft would create artificial gravity and help counteract the effects of such a long space flight. It will take longer to communicate with Earth as the spacecraft travels farther away. It could take up to 20-30 minutes for transmissions to reach the command centre on Earth.

Before the spacecraft enters the Martian atmosphere, the booster section will be jettisoned. The spacecraft then goes into orbit and prepares to descend to the surface. On reaching Mars, the four crew astronauts will be the first humans to stand on a planet other than Earth.

As the spacecraft approaches Mars after its long journey, the propulsion, or booster, stage is jettisoned, its fuel spent (below). It may be lost in deep space or sent to orbit around Mars to act as a communications relay station between the astronauts landed there and the command centre on Earth.

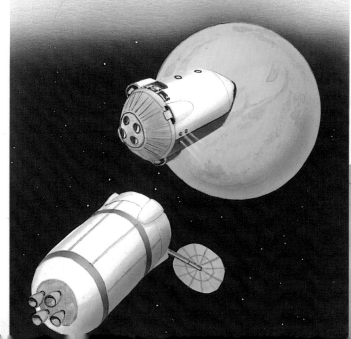

Return to Earth

Once their mission on Mars is completed, the astronauts will lift off from the surface using the fuel generated by the propellant plant. The Earth Return Vehicle (ERV) will probably have a total weight of 29 tonnes. A small nuclear reactor will be on board, producing 100 kilowatts of power to run the onboard systems for the six-month journey home. The habitation module and perhaps a second ERV would be left behind for the next crew.

Although Mars Direct and Mars Semi Direct are currently only in the planning stages, NASA mission designers say that a manned mission to the red planet *will* happen, probably before 2020.

After approximately 18 months on the surface, the astronauts will pack up their experiments and prepare to leave Mars. The inflatable modules will be stored in the habitation module left behind for future missions.

The spacecraft leaves Mars, propelled by fuel manufactured by the propellant plant during the mission.

Bringing Life to Mars

Mars is remarkably similar to Earth, although smaller and cooler. Both planets have a day length of about 24 hours, an important factor for plants taken to Mars that must adapt to their new environment. Mars' axis is also tilted at a degree similar to Earth's, and Mars has seasons. Some scientists believe that in the distant future it may be possible to transform Mars into a planet that resembles Earth and supports life – a process called terraforming. Greenhouse gases pumped into the Martian atmosphere would cause global warming. The polar ice caps would eventually melt and the water would create rivers and lakes. Terraforming Mars would take a long time – about 100 years of warming and another 500 years to melt the planet's underground ice. Bacteria and plants could be introduced from Earth so that eventually, after hundreds of years, they would grow naturally all over Mars.

An artist's impression of what the first Mars base camp might look like (below). The two habitation modules are connected by inflatable modules. Greenhouses for growing plants and food could be created in the same way.

Possibly, in the distant future, the Martian atmosphere could be warmed to Earth-like temperatures.

Scientists at this initial base would research the requirements of a larger settlement in the future.

These two images of Mars show what might happen if the surface temperature increases. Water released from the polar caps would collect in the lowland areas of the northern hemisphere to form a large ocean.

Humans could not breathe the Martian air, so oxygen tanks and masks would be needed to survive.

Glossary

Atmosphere
The layer of gases surrounding a planet.

Cosmonaut
The term used in Russia and the former USSR for an astronaut.

Elliptical orbit
The oval-shaped path an object makes as it travels around another object.

ESA
European Space Agency – the organisation responsible for space research in Europe.

Geology
The study of the structure and origin of rocks.

Hydrology
The study of the structure of water and its movement.

Interplanetary space
A term describing the space between planets.

Microbial life
Life forms so small that they can only be seen through a microscope or electron microscope, for example bacteria and single-celled algae.

NASA
National Aeronautics and Space Administration – the organisation responsible for space research in the USA.

Orbit
The curved path an object makes as it travels around another object.

Payload
A spacecraft's cargo.

Probe
A robot device controlled from Earth, designed to explore and study space.

Rover vehicle
A wheeled space vehicle designed to explore a planet's surface.

Solar flare
A burst of electrically charged particles (protons) from the sun.

Solar wind
A stream of electrically charged particles (protons) from the sun, 'blown' through the solar system.

Weightlessness
What astronauts experience in a spacecraft where the effect of gravity is not felt. They float as if they have no weight.

Mars Facts

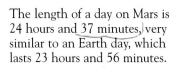

The length of a day on Mars is 24 hours and 37 minutes, very similar to an Earth day, which lasts 23 hours and 56 minutes.

It takes 687 days for Mars to orbit the sun, compared to Earth's 365 days.

Mars' distance from the sun is between 206 and 249 million km depending on its position in orbit.

Mars has seasons similar to Earth's – they are caused by the planet's elliptical orbit, tilted axis and its differing distance from the sun throughout the Martian year.

The minimum speed needed to escape a planet's gravitational pull is called the escape velocity. The escape velocity needed on Mars is 18,936 kph, less than half the 40,321 kph needed to leave Earth's gravity. Mars' gravity is only one-third that of Earth.

Mars is about half the size of Earth. Mars' diameter is 6,790 km while Earth's is 12,755 km.

Mars is a less dense planet than Earth and weighs about one-tenth of our world.

Mars has two moons, called Phobos and Deimos. They are named after the sons of the Greek god of war and mean 'fear' and 'terror' respectively.

The Martian moon Phobos is about 22 km in diameter. Both Phobos and Deimos are thought to have originally been asteroids that were captured by Mars' gravitational pull.

Dust storms on Mars can reach speeds of over 300 kph.

Due to the lack of air pressure on Mars, a 100-kph wind blowing there has the same effect as a 10-kph breeze on Earth.

The Valles Marineris is an awesome canyon that stretches about 4,500 km across Mars' surface. It is 10 km deep and 100 km across in places.

Olympus Mons on Mars is the largest known volcano in our solar system. It rises to almost 28 km and makes Mount Everest on Earth (8.9 km high) look like a foothill! The caldera, or opening on top, of Olympus Mons is about 90 km across and the base is about 550 km wide.

Mars' average surface temperature is -60 °C compared with Earth's average of 15°C.

Olympus Mons 28 km high

Mount Everest 8.9 km high

Chronology

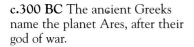

c.300 BC The ancient Greeks name the planet Ares, after their god of war.

c.50 BC The Romans rename the planet Mars, after their god of war.

1609 Johannes Kepler, a German mathematician, figures out that the orbit of Mars is elliptical using data collected by the Danish astronomer Tycho Brahe.

1877 Mars' two moons are discovered by American astronomer Asaph Hall.

1877 Giovanni Schiaparelli, an Italian astronomer, reports seeing strange dark areas on the surface of Mars and calls them *canali*.

1894 The American astronomer Percival Lowell makes many observations of Mars and concludes that there are canal systems and fertile vegetation there, all signs of a Martian race.

1898 H.G. Wells writes *War of the Worlds*, a science fiction novel about Martians taking over the Earth.

1917 Edgar Rice Burroughs writes the first of his series of 11 novels about Mars, *The Princess of Mars*.

1926 Walter Sydney Adams, a US astronomer, determines that Mars is ultra-arid (extremely dry).

1927 By analysing light through their telescope, William Webber Cablentz and Carl Otto Lampland measure differences between day and night temperatures on Mars. They believe this is a sign of a thin atmosphere.

1938 On 30th October, Orson Welles' broadcast of *War of the Worlds* causes panic throughout the USA when listeners think it is the real thing.

1965 US Mariner 4 is the first probe to successfully fly by Mars. It provides the first close-up pictures of another planet.

1969 Mariners 6 and 7 fly by Mars.

1971 The USSR's Mars 2 is the first Soviet orbiter to reach Mars and deploy a lander (which fails). The following Mars 3 lander reaches the planet and sends back the first panoramic image of the Martian surface.

1971-72 US Mariner 9 is the first successful Mars orbiter, taking over 7,000 pictures and providing our first real look at the planet and its moons.

1974 The USSR's Mars 4 is intended to orbit the planet but flies by when the retro-rocket fails to fire. Mars 5 makes a successful orbit. Mars 6 tries to land but loses communications contact before touchdown. Mars 7 flies by the planet and drops a lander, which misses the planet.

1976-1982 Viking 1, the US orbiter and lander, is a success and provides further pictures of the planet from the surface.

1976-1980 Viking 2, the second US probe, is a success. No signs of microbial life are found.

1988 Two USSR probes are sent to Mars: Phobos 1 and 2. Phobos 1 is unsuccessful, but Phobos 2 orbits the planet in 1989 and sends back pictures of the moon Phobos.

1992 NASA's Mars Observer probe is launched. Approaches the planet in August 1993 but control is lost before it can enter orbit.

1996 NASA scientists announce that tube-like structures found in a meteorite from Mars are fossils of organisms that once lived on the planet. However, later they agree with British scientists that although the tiny structures exist, they cannot be sure whether a living organism formed them.

1997 US Mars Pathfinder lands using an inflated ball procedure, bouncing across the surface. On board is Sojourner, the first wheeled vehicle to explore another planet.

1997-98 Mars Global Surveyor maps the planet from 350 km above the surface and studies the weather.

1998 The Japanese probe Nozomi blasts off and goes off course, but is now on target to reach Mars in 2004.

1999 Mars Climate Orbiter reaches the planet after an 11-month journey, but due to miscalculations by NASA scientists, it gets too close to enter correct orbit.

1999 Mars Polar Lander ready for touchdown in December but its thrusters malfunction and make its landing unsuccessful.

2001 NASA's 2001 Mars Odyssey spacecraft goes into orbit around Mars as scheduled on 24th October. It will map minerals and elements.

2003 Mars Express, ESA's first mission to Mars, is due to be launched. It will have a British-designed lander on board called Beagle 2.

2005 Mars Surveyor 2005 could be the first mission to return a sample from the planet's surface to Earth.

2005, 2007 or 2009 (Date as yet undecided.) Master, an ESA craft, will drop a lander on Mars before continuing on its journey to an asteroid.

2015-20 Possibility of a manned mission to explore Mars.

Index